COMEDY OF BLESSINGS

LAUGH, CRY, SMH - MY JOURNEY AS A CAREGIVER & THE A.R.K METHOD

CARLA HENRY-LEWIS

CONTENTS

DEDICATION

To my parents, Dr. Lloyd N. Henry MD and Carolyn Winfrey Henry.

From the depths of my heart, I extend my gratitude for the invaluable lessons you've imparted to me. Hen, you taught me the essence of common sense, the importance of treating everyone equally, and the wisdom of never engaging in fruitless arguments. Your teachings have been the guiding light in my journey.

Mommy, you were a trailblazer, a woman ahead of her time. From you, I inherited my creative spark and practical approach to life. Your multifaceted talents, from crafting beautiful classroom bulletin boards to orchestrating grand musicals, from building sturdy decks to designing intricate irrigation systems, have always left me in awe. Your spirit and resilience inspire me every day. I love you.

To my siblings, LaVerne, Carmen, Letitia, and Lloyd, life's journey is all the more enriching and joyful with you by my side.

To my husband, Zac, this is for our future, for the days of relaxation and retirement that await us.

To my precious daughters, Rebekah, Tabitha, and Hannah, thank you for grounding me, for the laughter, the challenges, and the memories. You remind me every day of the beauty in simplicity and the strength in love.

And to my darling granddaughter, Elizabeth, "hugga mugga." May you always find joy in the little moments and know that you are cherished beyond measure.

INTRODUCTION

FINDING LAUGHTER IN LIFE'S UNEXPECTED MOMENTS

"A day without laughter is a day wasted."

— CHARLIE CHAPLIN

Have you ever found yourself in a situation so absurd, so utterly unexpected, that all you could do was laugh? Or perhaps you've faced challenges that seemed insurmountable, only to find a silver lining in the form of a comedic twist? Welcome to the world of *Comedy of Blessings*, where we embrace the unexpected, find humor in the mundane, and celebrate the joyous moments that life throws our way.

I'm Carla, and my journey as a caregiver has been nothing short of a rollercoaster. From the heartwarming moments of shared laughter to the tearful nights of uncertainty, I've experienced it all. But amidst the chaos, I discovered a powerful tool that helped me navigate these challenges with grace and humor: the

A.R.K. Method. This book is my attempt to share this method, my experiences, and the countless comedic moments that have brightened my days.

So, why did I write this book? Because I believe that laughter is not just the best medicine; it's a beacon of hope. In the face of adversity, it's easy to feel overwhelmed, lost, and alone. But by embracing humor, we can find solace, connect with others, and, most importantly, rediscover the joy in our journey. Through *Comedy of Blessings*, I aim to offer a fresh perspective on caregiving, one that focuses not on the burdens but on the blessings.

As you delve into these pages, you'll be introduced to the A.R.K. Method. This structured approach addresses the primary drivers in caregiving: the need for *Acknowledgment*, the desire to be *Right or Respected*, and the quest for *Knowledge*, as well as the corresponding emotions: *Anger, Resentment,* and *Keen Disappointment*. But more than just a method, A.R.K. is a philosophy, one that champions *Awareness, Relationships*, and *Kindness*. Together, we'll explore how these principles can transform your caregiving experience, turning challenges into opportunities for growth, connection, and laughter.

But this book is more than just a guide; it's a celebration. A celebration of the comedic moments that punctuate our lives, the relationships that sustain us, and the blessings that often come from the most unexpected places. Through personal anecdotes, heartwarming stories, and practical advice, I'll share the lessons I've learned, the laughter I've shared, and the tools that have helped me navigate the complex world of caregiving.

So, what can you expect from *Comedy of Blessings?* Expect to laugh, to cry, and to shake your head in disbelief. Expect to be inspired, to feel empowered, and to see caregiving in a whole new light. But most importantly, expect to discover the joy behind every situation and to value the precious moments that life offers.

As we embark on this journey together, I invite you to embrace the comedy of blessings. To find humor in the everyday, to cherish the relationships that enrich our lives, and to approach caregiving with an open heart and a hearty laugh. For in the end, it's not the challenges we face but the way we meet them that defines our experience.

And now, as we transition into the heart of this book, let's dive deep into the A.R.K. Method, exploring its principles, its benefits, and its transformative power. Let's embark on a journey of laughter, love, and learning, and together, let's discover the comedy of blessings that awaits us all.

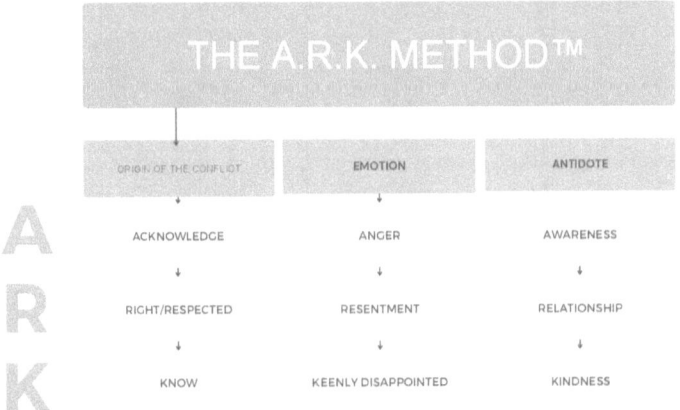

ABOUT THE AUTHOR

In the vibrant tapestry of life, some individuals stand out, not just for their achievements but for their spirit, resilience, and the stories they weave. One such individual is Carla Henry Lewis, the author of "Comedy of Blessings."

Born as the second child among five, Carla was, in many ways, destined to be a caregiver. From the sun-kissed shores of St. Croix to the bustling streets of Maywood, IL, her journey has been punctuated with moments of laughter, tears, and profound realizations. Whether it was administering an insulin shot to Gramme at a tender age or navigating the intricate dance of relationships, she has always approached challenges with a unique blend of humor, authenticity, and empowerment.

Her mantra, "In the midst of challenges, find your stage," encap sulates her approach to life. It's about embracing strengths, celebrating achievements, and finding humor even in the most unexpected places. Her journey with her spouse, Zachary, and her adventures in caregiving, whether it was tending to a garden or supporting a 'bionic' mother through her recovery, are testaments to her indomitable spirit.

But beyond the stories and the anecdotes lies a soul that believes in the power of connection, the magic of kindness, and the beauty of authenticity. Through "*Comedy of Blessings*," she invites you to step into her world, to find your own stage amidst challenges, and to embrace life with all its ups and downs.

Carla is also the acclaimed author of "The Key to Overcoming Conflict," the first in her transformative "Stress Makeover" series. She's on a mission to provide simple, practical ways to manage stress in any situation. Her passion for empowering others shines through in every word she writes and every workshop she conducts.

Stay connected with Carla and embark on a journey of self-discovery, laughter, and resilience. Follow her on Instagram and Facebook @coachcarlahenrylewis or visit her website at www.carlahenrylewis.com.

In her words, "Let's rise above the digital noise and celebrate our real, messy, beautiful lives." So, dear reader, as you delve into the pages of this book, remember that every challenge, every tear, and every laugh line is a badge of honor, a testament to the comedy of blessings that life bestows upon us.

1

DIVING DEEP INTO THE A.R.K. METHOD

"Any fool can know. The point is to understand."

— ALBERT EINSTEIN

I n the vast tapestry of life, there are threads that bind us, patterns that define us, and colors that bring vibrancy to our existence. As caregivers, we often find ourselves weaving intricate patterns, trying to balance our responsibilities, emotions, and the ever-evolving dynamics of our relationships. But amidst this complexity, there's a method, a guiding principle, that can help us navigate with grace, understanding, and a touch of humor. Welcome to the A.R.K. Method.

UNDERSTANDING THE PRIMARY DRIVERS:

Acknowledgment: Picture this: You've spent hours, days, perhaps even years, dedicating yourself to the wellbeing of a loved one.

You've sacrificed sleep, personal time, and often, your own needs. And in those quiet moments, when exhaustion threatens to overwhelm, a simple word of appreciation, a nod of acknowledgment, can make all the difference. It's not about seeking validation but about feeling seen and recognized in your role. As caregivers, our journey is often silent, our efforts behind the scenes. But the need for acknowledgment is real, and it's profound. It's a gentle reminder that our actions matter and that our love and dedication have value.

Right or Respect: Respect is a two-way street. As caregivers, we pour our hearts into making the right decisions for our loved ones. We research, we consult, we deliberate. But beyond the practicalities, there's an emotional aspect to it: the desire to be understood, to be respected for our choices, and to be trusted in our decisions. It's about navigating the delicate balance between our role as caregivers and our identity as individuals. It's about asserting our voice, standing our ground, and, most importantly, ensuring that our loved ones receive the best care possible.

Knowledge: The realm of caregiving is vast and often uncharted. From medical terminologies to legal intricacies, the quest for knowledge is relentless. But it's not just about gathering information; it's about understanding, about gaining clarity in our responsibilities. It's about equipping ourselves with the tools and insights to provide the best care, anticipate challenges, and be proactive in our approach. Knowledge empowers us, gives us confidence, and ensures that we're always a step ahead in our caregiving journey.

THE RESULTING EMOTIONS:

Anger: It's a raw, visceral emotion, often bubbling beneath the surface. When our efforts go unnoticed, when our decisions are questioned, or when we feel overwhelmed, anger can rear its head. It's a natural response to feeling unappreciated or misunderstood. But here's the thing about anger: It's not the enemy. It's a signal, a red flag, indicating deeper issues that need addressing. Through the A.R.K. Method, we'll explore ways to channel this emotion, to understand its roots, and to transform it into a force for positive change.

Resentment: It's the slow-burning ember, the emotion that lingers long after the initial spark. Resentment often stems from continuous challenges without acknowledgment, from feeling undervalued or overlooked. It's the silent weight that can cloud our judgment, strain our relationships, and dampen our spirits. But like anger, resentment is a sign, a call to action. It's an invitation to communicate, to seek understanding, and to rebuild bridges.

Keen Disappointment: We've all been there. The moments when reality falls short of expectations, when hopes are dashed, and dreams seem distant. In caregiving, keen disappointment can arise when our efforts don't yield the desired results, when our loved ones face setbacks, or when the journey becomes too daunting. But here's the silver lining: Disappointment, though painful, can be a catalyst for growth. It challenges us to reassess, to adapt, and to find new ways to approach our caregiving journey.

As we delve deeper into the A.R.K. Method in the chapters ahead, I invite you to embrace these emotions, to understand their origins, and to use them as stepping stones toward a more fulfilling, joyful, and empowered caregiving experience. Remember, in the comedy of blessings, every emotion, every challenge, and every moment has its place. And together, we'll navigate this journey with humor, grace, and a whole lot of heart.

2

AWARENESS IN CAREGIVING EMBRACING THE DANCE OF EMOTIONS

"The deepest craving of human nature is the need to be appreciated."

— WILLIAM JAMES

In the radiant glow of twilight, I sat beside my father, a resilient soul in his 80s, recovering from yet another health episode. This wasn't our first rodeo; it was the second signifi cant health scare in just two years. And as if the universe was testing my strength, I was thrown into the deep end earlier when my mom needed both knee and hip replacements. But here's the thing: amidst the whirlwind of emotions and respon- sibilities, I found clarity, strength, and, yes, even humor. Welcome to the dance of caregiving, where every step is a lesson, every twirl an emotion, and every leap a testament to our strength.

RECOGNIZING EMOTIONS:

As caregivers navigating the workplace jungle, our days are often a blur of tasks. Medications, appointments, comfort measures it's a nonstop hustle. But beneath this hustle lies a realm of emotions as vast and varied as the stars. From the highs of hope to the lows of despair, our hearts experience it all. Recognizing these emotions? That's where the magic happens. It's not just about self-awareness; it's about empowerment. By embracing our feelings, we not only understand ourselves better but also find the strength to navigate challenges with grace and authenticity.

NAVIGATING CHALLENGES WITH PERSPECTIVE:

Life's got a quirky sense of humor, throwing curveballs when we least expect them. But here's where our brand of comedy shines. With awareness as our compass, we can shift our perspective, finding humor in the most unexpected places. Remember the time when mom, postsurgery, joked about her 'bionic leg'? That wasn't just a quip; it was a moment of empowerment, a testament to her indomitable spirit. It's these moments, these nuggets of humor, that transform our caregiving journey from a challenge to a celebration.

PERSONAL ANECDOTES: DANCING IN THE GARDEN OF MEMORIES

Life has a funny way of setting the stage for us, even in the most unexpected places. Take, for instance, my father's garden in St.

Croix. After his health scare, his primary concern wasn't the myriad of medical appointments or the medications. No, it was his garden. His precious plants beckoned, and he fretted over them, even from miles away.

So, there I was, amidst the dry, barren soil of Dad's cherished ⅛ acre land, tending to his beloved pineapples. Now, let me be clear: manual labor and I aren't the best of friends. But for Dad? I'd dance in the dirt and sing to the plants. Each weed pulled, and every drop of water sprinkled became an act of love, a tribute to the countless memories we'd built over the years. It was laughter, tears, and a dance of nostalgia all rolled into one.

Then there's Mom, truly my bionic marvel. After her surgeries, she didn't merely take tentative steps; she danced her way through therapy sessions. Remarkably, she often chose not to rely on her pain medication, fearing the shadow of addiction. Her resilience was awe-inspiring. With each determined step, she embodied the belief that challenges aren't insurmountable barriers; they're simply stepping stones, gateways to new opportunities and growth. Her journey was a testament to the strength of the human spirit, proving that with grit and grace, any hurdle can be transformed into a dance of triumph.

These moments, these personal stories, are the essence of my caregiving journey. They serve as a testament to the power of perspective, the magic of humor, and the boundless depths of love. Through them, I've come to realize that every challenge, every hurdle, can be transformed into a comedy of blessings with the right mindset and a heart full of love.

So, as we step into the next chapter, I invite you to join me in this dance of caregiving. Embrace your emotions, find humor in the unexpected, and remember that in our comedy of blessings, every challenge is just a step in our dance.

3

BUILDING AND FOSTERING RELATIONSHIPS THE DANCE OF CONNECTION

"Each friend represents a world in us, a world possibly not born until they arrive, and it is only by this meeting that a new world is born."

ANAIS NIN

In the intricate ballet of life, relationships are the choreography that gives our journey rhythm, grace, and purpose. As caregivers, we often find ourselves at the crossroads, juggling our responsibilities with the delicate dance of relationships. But here's the beautiful part: every step, every twirl, every leap in this dance is an opportunity to connect, to understand, and to find strength in unity.

THE POWER OF CONNECTION:

Imagine standing in the center of a vast ballroom, the spotlight on you. As the music begins, you're not alone; partners surround you, each one ready to join you in the dance. This is the power of connection. Having relationships with family, friends, or support groups can offer a lifeline, a source of strength, understanding, and validation. They remind us that even in the most challenging moments of caregiving, we're not dancing solo. We have a troupe, a community that's with us every step of the way, cheering us on, lifting us up, and celebrating our journey.

NAVIGATING RELATIONSHIPS IN CAREGIVING:

Like any dance, the choreography of relationships in caregiving can be complex. How do we balance our role as caregivers with our relationships? How do we ensure that while we're taking care of our loved ones, our relationships don't take a backseat? It's about setting boundaries, communicating openly, and, most importantly, embracing the dance. It's about recognizing that while caregiving is a significant part of our journey, it's not the entirety. Our relationships, our connections, are the melodies that add joy, depth, and richness to our lives.

PERSONAL STORIES: THE JOYS AND CHALLENGES OF MAINTAINING RELATIONSHIPS WHILE CAREGIVING

One such story takes me back to my teenage years when I was entrusted with the responsibility of caring for my maternal grandmother, Thelma Winfrey, AKA Gramme. A spirited lady from Maywood, IL, Gramme, had diabetes and required regular insulin injections. I still remember the trepidation I felt the first time I had to administer her insulin. The needle, the anticipation, and the responsibility weighed heavily on my young shoulders. But it was also a moment of profound connection, a realization of the depth of my role in her life.

Fast forward to a few years later, and I found myself once again in the role of a caregiver, this time for my spouse, Zachary. Our honeymoon in the Poconos was overshadowed by his sudden illness, marking the beginning of a tumultuous journey filled with hospital visits, medical challenges, and emotional roller-coasters. But amidst the chaos, there were moments of clarity, of humor, and of profound love. Like the time a nurse mistook me for Zachary's mother, a moment that brought a chuckle to his face (not mine, lol. I had an aha moment. I'm not about to die first and let some other woman raise my kids 😊).

LAUGHTER, TEARS, AND SHARED MOMENTS

"Life's most persistent and urgent question is, 'What are you doing for others?'"

— MARTIN LUTHER KING JR.

As we navigate this enlightening journey together, I hope you've found moments of laughter, tears, and profound insights that resonate with your own experiences. Your engagement and reflections are invaluable, not just to me but to countless others who are on a similar path.

Have you found a particular story or lesson that touched your heart? Or perhaps a strategy that you believe will change your approach to caregiving? I invite you to share these moments and insights. Consider this an exclusive opportunity to be a beacon for others, guiding them through their journeys with your words.

Your thoughts, experiences, and reflections can be a guiding light for someone else. I encourage you to take a moment to share your insights on Amazon. Your words have the power to inspire, uplift, and provide solace to someone else in need.

Thank you for being an integral part of this journey. Let's continue to find the comedy in our blessings together.

Leave a review

4

KINDNESS AS THE HEART OF CAREGIVING THE SYMPHONY OF COMPASSION

"You cannot do a kindness too soon because you never know how soon it will be too late."

— RALPH WALDO EMERSON

In the grand orchestra of life, kindness is the melody that resonates, touches hearts, and creates ripples of positivity. As caregivers, we're often at the forefront of this symphony, orchestrating acts of kindness, compassion, and love. But here's the beautiful part: every note, every chord, every crescendo in this symphony is an opportunity to make a difference, to touch a heart, and to spread joy.

THE RIPPLE EFFECT OF KINDNESS:

Imagine dropping a pebble into a serene pond. The ripples spread, touching every corner, every nook and cranny. This is the power of kindness. A simple act, a word of encouragement, a gesture of love, can create ripples that spread far and wide. As caregivers, our acts of kindness not only uplift our loved ones but also inspire others, creating a chain reaction of positivity, understanding, and love.

PRACTICING KINDNESS TO ONESELF:

But here's the thing about the symphony of caregiving: while we're busy creating melodies of kindness for others, we often forget to compose a tune for ourselves. Self-care, self-compassion, and self-love are the notes that add depth, richness, and harmony to our caregiving journey. It's about recognizing that while we're dedicated to our loved ones, we, too, deserve kindness, love, and care. It's about taking a moment to pause, reflect, and indulge in acts of self-kindness, whether it's a spa day, a quiet evening with a book, or simply a moment of meditation.

PERSONAL ANECDOTES: HEARTWARMING STORIES OF KINDNESS IN ACTION

Kindness, they say, is the language that the deaf can hear and the blind can see. In the realm of caregiving, kindness takes on a whole new dimension, offering solace, hope, and moments of pure magic.

One such moment takes me back to the time when my father, in his 80s, suffered two significant health episodes within two years. The first incident, a heart attack, saw him being airlifted to Miami for life-saving surgery. The ordeal, though harrowing, was also a testament to the resilience of the human spirit and the power of collective hope. Here is the link to the article about this incident, which serves as a poignant reminder of the fragility and beauty of life.

Story of Dr. Henry

The second episode, a stroke, brought with it its own set of challenges. But even in the face of adversity, there were moments of humor, like when my mother prioritized cleaning him up over calling 911. It's these moments, these unexpected bursts of laughter, that make the caregiving journey genuinely unique.

And then there's the story of my paternal grandmother, Ingerborg Henry. A nonagenarian with dementia, her spirit remained undeterred. The image of her, in her 90s, attempting to climb over a locked gate with the help of a chair is both heartwarming and hilarious. It's a testament to the indomitable spirit of older adults and the moments of pure comedy that punctuate the caregiving journey.

5

LAUGHTER, TEARS, AND THE CAREGIVER'S JOURNEY THE DANCE OF EMOTIONS

"Celebrate the small things and our lives become bigger than ever."

— ANONYMOUS

In the grand theater of life, every caregiver has a unique story to tell, a dance of emotions that oscillates between laughter and tears. It's a journey filled with unexpected twists, turns, and moments that leave an indelible mark on our hearts. But here's the beautiful part: every step, every twirl, every leap in this dance is an opportunity to find joy, to heal, and to celebrate.

FINDING HUMOR IN THE UNEXPECTED:

Imagine navigating the workplace jungle of caregiving, and amidst the challenges, you stumble upon a moment of pure, unadulterated humor. It could be a loved one's quirky comment, a hilarious mixup, or simply a lighthearted moment that breaks the monotony. Embracing these moments and finding humor in the unexpected is the key to adding a touch of sunshine to our caregiving journey. It's a reminder that even in the most challenging situations, there's always a reason to smile, laugh, and cherish the comedy of blessings.

THE THERAPEUTIC NATURE OF TEARS:

Tears, often seen as a sign of weakness, are in fact, the soul's way of healing, processing emotions, and finding clarity. As caregivers, we're no strangers to tears of frustration, of joy, of relief, and sometimes, of sheer exhaustion. But here's the silver lining: every tear is a testament to our strength, our resilience, and our unwavering dedication. It's about permitting ourselves to feel, to process, and to heal. It's about embracing the therapeutic nature of tears and recognizing them as a vital part of our caregiving journey.

CELEBRATING SMALL VICTORIES: RECOGNIZING AND APPRECIATING THE WINS, NO MATTER HOW SMALL

Every caregiver's journey is punctuated with moments of triumph, moments that deserve to be celebrated and cherished.

For me, one such moment was when my mother, Carolyn, underwent hip and knee replacement surgeries. The surgeries, though challenging, also brought with them moments of triumph, resilience, and profound connection. Whether it was her recuperation at my home in AL or her physical therapy sessions in Florida and St. Croix, every step of the journey was a testament to her indomitable spirit and our collective strength as a family.

6

TOOLS AND RESOURCES FOR THE MODERN CAREGIVER NAVIGATING THE LABYRINTH WITH GRACE

"We become what we behold. We shape our tools, and thereafter our tools shape us."

— MARSHALL MCLUHAN

I n the digital age, the world of caregiving has transformed, offering a plethora of tools, resources, and platforms that empower, educate, and support caregivers. But with this abundance comes the challenge of navigating, finding the right tools, and building a support system that resonates with our unique needs.

NAVIGATING THE WORLD OF CAREGIVING:

From apps that track medications to online forums that offer advice, the modern caregiver has a treasure trove of resources at their fingertips. But how do we navigate this world? How do we find tools that align with our needs? It's about research, seeking recommendations, and, most importantly, about staying updated. This guide will offer insights into essential resources, tools, and platforms that can transform the caregiving journey, making it more efficient, informed, and empowered.

BUILDING A SUPPORT SYSTEM: THE IMPORTANCE OF COMMUNITY AND SEEKING HELP

The caregiving journey, though deeply personal, is also a collective one. It's a journey that requires a robust support system, a tribe that offers support, understanding, and moments of respite. My journey as a caregiver has been enriched by the presence of my family, a tribe that has stood by me through thick and thin. Whether it was my role as a caregiver for my grandparents, my spouse, or my parents, my family has been my pillar of strength, offering support, understanding, and moments of pure joy.

SELF-CARE FOR THE CAREGIVER:

Amidst the hustle and bustle of caregiving, it's easy to forget the most crucial person ourselves. Self-care, often relegated to the backburner, is in fact, the cornerstone of a successful caregiving journey. It's about prioritizing our well-being, about taking breaks, and about indulging in activities that rejuvenate and refresh. Whether it's a spa day, a quiet evening with a book, or simply a walk in the park, self-care is the key to staying balanced, focused, and energized in our caregiving journey.

TOGETHER, WE CREATE A SYMPHONY OF STORIES

As we reach the culmination of our shared journey, I hope you've been armed with tools, stories, and perspectives that will enrich your caregiving experience. Every story, every lesson, and every moment of reflection adds a unique note to the symphony of caregiving stories.

Your journey, your insights, and your reflections are a treasure trove waiting to be shared. Consider this a golden opportunity to add your unique note to this symphony. Your experiences can inspire, guide, and uplift someone else on a similar path.

WE WANT TO HEAR FROM YOU!

IF YOU ENJOYED THIS BOOK, PLEASE LEAVE A REVIEW TO HELP OTHERS

We value your opinion deeply. Your voice matters. I invite you to share your reflections, insights, and experiences on Amazon. Let your words be the guiding star for someone else navigating the intricate dance of caregiving.

Thank you for being a cherished part of this narrative. Together, we create a tapestry of stories, each thread invaluable and irreplaceable.

Leave a review

CONCLUSION

EMBRACING THE FUTURE WITH THE A.R.K. METHOD THE GRAND FINALE OF OUR DANCE

 "Hope is being able to see that there is light despite all of the darkness."

— DESMOND TUTU

As we come to the end of our shared journey through the pages of *"Comedy of Blessings,"* let's take a moment to bask in the afterglow of our dance. It was a dance that was filled with laughter, tears, challenges, victories, and countless shared moments. It was choreographed with the empowering rhythms of the A.R.K. Method."

REFLECTING ON THE JOURNEY:

Navigating the realm of caregiving, we embarked on a transformative journey, discovering the power of Awareness, the beauty of Relationships, and the magic of Kindness. We delved deep into our emotions, finding strength in vulnerability, humor in the unexpected, and joy in the smallest of moments. We celebrated our victories, no matter how tiny, and found solace in our shared experiences. As we stand at this juncture, let's take a moment to reflect on the key takeaways, the lessons learned, and the memories cherished.

LOOKING AHEAD WITH HOPE AND HUMOR:

The road ahead, though uncertain, is filled with promise. With the A.R.K. Method as our compass, we're not just equipped to navigate challenges; we're empowered to transform them into opportunities. There are many opportunities to connect, to learn, and to grow. So, as we step into the future, let's do so with hope in our hearts and humor in our steps. Let's remember that every challenge is just a step in our dance, every setback an opportunity to twirl, and every moment a chance to shine.

A CALL TO ACTION:

But our dance doesn't end here. It's a continuous journey, a dance that evolves with every step, every experience, and every shared moment. I invite you, dear reader, to embrace the A.R.K. Method in your own life. We can find strength in Awareness, joy in Relationships, and magic in Kindness. And as you do, share your stories, your moments, and your victories with others. Let's create a ripple effect, a symphony of caregiving stories that inspire, uplift, and empower. Because in the grand theater of life, every story, every dance, and every moment is a testament to our strength, our resilience, and our unwavering spirit.

With this, we conclude our journey through "*Comedy of Blessings*." But remember, every ending is just a new beginning. So, as you step into the future, do so with grace, with hope, and with the empowering rhythms of the A.R.K. Method guiding your every step.

www.ingramcontent.com/pod-product-compliance
Lightning Source LLC
Chambersburg PA
CBHW030528130626
46549CB00007B/3139